The secret of the rich

The most inspirational book ever

written on wealth.

SUNIL KUMAR GUPTA (MAHAGURU)

Editor: Sanjay Gupta

The secret

of
the rich

This book will take you from zero to peak and from poverty to richness.

This describes the mysterious theories of ancient economics and modern life philosophy.

Editor: Sanjay Gupta

Copyright © 2019 Sunil Kumar Gupta (Mahaguru)

All rights reserved.

Immense devotion and unlimited dedication

This book is dedicated to my revered father Shri Om Prakash Gupta ji.

He lost everything due to his stupidity and became poor. Because of his stupidity, I got inspiration to write this book.

"My words are not of mine, but of my father And my father never lied."

Jesus Christ

"Also I heard God say, whom should I send and who will go by our side? Then I said, I am ready, send me."
(Isaiah 6: 8)

"Now go, write in front of them and keep it the book, that it is important for this time, it is important to be forever." (Isaiah 30: 8)

Get up, wake up
And open your eyes,
see your Savior has come.

Introduction

The author of this book, Sunil Kumar Gupta (Mahaguru), is a

successful businessman. It is a knower of economics, business science, ethics, modern life philosophy and sociology. They also have good knowledge of public behavior.

It is born in a city of a businessman, Azamgarh (India). Since its caste was a businessman, its family environment was of business. For this reason, he was acquiring good knowledge of business since his childhood and became a successful businessman when he was young. It is currently living in his native place Azamgarh (India). He wrote "the secret of the rich" from his earlier experiences and intensive studies. Who is fully capable of making a person rich. This book will lead people from zero to peak and from poverty to prosperity.

Please share this book with the poor people and motivate them to read this book. If you really want to help a relative and a well wisher, then give this book in the gift.

Here I request the bank employees / officers and the insurance employees / officers that they should inform their clients and borrowers about this book, not only the information but also encourage them to read this book.

This book will reach the summit of popularity in a very short time, and one day will become a historical treatise. I hope you enjoy reading this book and will take advantage of it.

Best wishes

Use these tools to contact the author.

Facebook@333sunilkumargupta

Twitter@iAmMahaguru

Instagram@sunilkumargupta
777

Unreal is interesting and fun. But in the opposite, the truth is curt and bitter. Think of this truth that without any business, no person can be rich. If there is a miracle then the thing is different.

SUNIL KUMAR GUPTA (MAHARURU)

A short story

A person who was very poor and had no degree with him. He thought, let's start a peon job in a company. This will be a resort to the survival and nurture of my family.

Then they put applications in many companies. A few days later, a company accepted their application and invited them for an interview.

On arrival, the interviewers took their practical exams first, and said "Make tea for all the people and we want to see if you can make tea properly or not. Upon hearing this, the person brought tea for all the people at the order of the interviewers and all the people drank tea. Tea liked all the people very much.

After this interviewers asked the person "What is your email id ?".

So the person said that "I do not have any email ID, I have not created any email ID till date", the interviewers said "how can you get this job" and that person in that company Peon's job was not found.

When that person came out of the company, he started worrying about his children's school fees and food. After that the person checked his pocket and he had seven dollars in one pocket, and he bought potato of seven dollars and kept it in the basket, went to people's home and started selling. All his potatoes were sold till the evening and his seven dollars, ten dollars Were turned into.

After that the person continued that business, and he continued this process continuously. Slowly the time was passing, and with the passage of time, his business was also growing.

The person first opened a shop of a daily commodity and then another shop, then another shop after that. In this way, that person became the owner of many shopping malls.

After that, when the person became a popular trader, one day his interview was taken on TV and interviewers from that person were asked, "What is your email id?"

So the person said that "I do not have any email ID, I have not created any email ID till date.

After listening to this answer, the authors asked the person with astonishment, "When you do not have any email ID, how did you set such a big business?"

The person reassured, again, that "I have made such a big business with my hard work and my own discretion".

So this short story gives us the inspiration: *"Whatever we have, it is very much. We should use it with great faith and discretion and not cry over our power.*

Subject-matter

1-To become rich, business is needed.

2- Money is needed for business.

3-Money is prepared by saving money.

4-How to save money?

5-How to trade?

6-What is the secret of the rich?

7-What to do to stay rich forever?

8- Do not ever do this to become rich.

9- Rich formula for people with a job.

10- Whatever you do to be rich, keep moving forward. Please note, think big.

I now accept God as a witness,
by his order, in the book I
am giving the inform.

Now we will keep our first step in the first chapter of prosperity.

Success does not get in one day but yes one day it definitely gets.

Best wishes

1

To become rich, business is needed.

There are many ways to become rich in this world. Some of them are right and some are wrong. Let's choose the right path.

Guilt route

What is the result of following the crime route? You guys know this well and understand it well. For example, I am writing a true incident of my city here. Three persons used to work on a wealthy businessman's shop. He kidnapped his own master's son to become rich and demanded one crore rupees for the ransom. After this, when the investigation of the police started, the three men were horrified and killed their master's son. And finally the three were caught by the police and the three people were jailed.

In this way they were not able to become rich, but yes the jail went on.

Savings route

Some people use the savings route to become rich, they sell their everything, break their business, deposit money in the bank, but they can not be rich enough. The bank will double our money in nine-ten years.

Now I am not able to understand the emptiness of such a slow pace. What do you guys understand?

Fraudulent route

If you want to be rich with fraud, then you can cheat someone at once. But once the person gets cheated he will be careful. After that the person or the other person will hardly get trapped in your trap. And once you betray someone, hardly you can become rich. Finally, art is needed to deceive.

And this art does not come to all people. I do not know this art at all and you know yourself.

Job path

Some people choose to get a job path to become rich. Which is true to some extent. If you get a big salary job then, okay, otherwise all your life will go through financial constraints. And hardly you can get rich by job.

This passage looks suspicious and dubious to me.

Gaming passage

When you bet in horse racing, do you know which horse is going to win? Or when you guys play cards, do you know which player has a card?

Do you people remember Mahabharata's Dharmaraj Yudhishtir? Always remember them while playing gambling

This route is also completely surrounded by darkness.

Now, in the end, only one way remains and that is the trade route. Yes you guys heard the right "trade route".

Yes you people have heard right that "to become rich, there is a need to do business.

You can tell me that if the late Mr. Jamshed Tata (the big industrialist of India) and the late Mr. Dhirubhai Ambani (the big businessman of India) had not done his business then could he become rich? And is he counted among the richest people of this nation and the world? And could the late Mr. Jamshed Tata, Tata Company and Late Shri Dhirubhai Ambani, build Reliance Company?

It is therefore mandatory to do business to be rich.

Unless you do your business, you can not be rich.

The way to reach the rich treasure is trade, business is the valley of diamonds, yes-yes the diamond valley.

Can you tell me that how much money will be invested in Reliance Industries and Tata companies to start their own company? So you will say to me, "He has a million rupees or one crore rupees. That would have been enough, not more than that ".

But now I want to tell you people that "Do not know how many millions of rupees Reliance Industries and Tata companies will have given their employees the wages and not knowing how many millions will be donated.

Now you can predict that companies like Reliance Industries and Tata companies are operating in total profits. And now you may have been aware of why I am saying that trade is a diamond valley.

You will also be surprised to know that all eighty percent of the world's people have only twenty percent of the money in this world. And only twenty percent of the world's people have eighty percent of the world's wealth.

Do you think this is true of people but this is true, like true gold is the truth.

Now, let us also know in clear and truthful words that only twenty percent of traders have eighty percent of the money in this world.

If you do not step in the business world then you can not be rich in dreams, leave it to the reality.

Every future possibilities of life are related to business. Trade is a good way to become immovable and safe in a safe way.

You should do business without any doubt and fear.

Some people come out with an excuse that "we do not have money, so how can we trade?"

But do not worry too much, you will be told in the next chapter that how capital is created for business and how money is made for business. In the next chapter, you will end up with the excuse of not having money and capital. And further chapters I will tell you guys how, how the capital is made.

***

2

Money is needed for business.

Today's round is a period of capitalist, we can not run a moment even without a capital. If the nation's renowned companies do not have money, can they make their own company?

Without money, we can not get clothes, medicine and food.

A person's dream was to become a very big man and a very big dealer, but because of his poverty, he could not make anything because he had no money.

And now you must have understood that without money we can not stand our business and when we can not stand our business then how can we become rich?

The great statesman Chanakya said in his statement and wrote in the great book Kautilya economics written by him that "doing something without money is like extracting oil from sand."

So you have now become clear that doing anything without money is like extracting oil from the sand.

How many patients die without treatment due to lack of capital, millions of people die from hunger every year due to lack of money.

You know that money is called meaning, because it means life, when we have money, then only we will understand the meaning of life correctly. Otherwise, the meaning of Deepawali, Dusshera, Holi and any festival will not be understood without money. When we have money, we will understand the meaning of life itself.

The vehicle runs from petrol, but the carriage of life runs through money only. And walking without a life of money is completely impossible.

In this topic I am telling you a true incident "A woman from my neighborhood, whose name was Mrs. Shalini Singh. Her husband had just departed from this world a few years ago. He has a son and a daughter who studies in college. He thought of making a clothing shop for his son Vikas Singh. But their thinking, this dream remained the same. Which could never be true Because they did not have the money to do all this and neither could they ever get it.

Well, how could a woman open her shop when she did not have the money.

Similarly, when we do not have money, how can we do our business?

A person whose name was Madan Saxena. One who ran a auto-rickshaw, had two daughters, the elder daughter's name was Riya and the younger daughter was Priya. Riya was ten years old and Priya was seven years old. Riya's four and Priya studied in class one. This dream of Madan Saxena was that I should make my two daughters as doctors. But alas, their dream could not be fulfilled. Because he did not have the money to read his two daughters and make a doctor.

None of our dreams can be fulfilled without money.

A boy named Amit Bhatia, who was studying in high school. Whose only dream was to become a manager by M.B.A., but he could not become M.B.A. because he had no money.

So you people saw that people can not do anything without money. Without money, we can not even move one step and a moment can not survive.

Every single dream of ours breaks every moment of money, and no one can fulfill our dreams without money.

In life, we need money on a step-by-step basis. We also need money for food. Money is also needed for clothes and medicines. We also need money for the education of our sons, marriage and buying or making a house.

***

3

Money is prepared by saving money

No person can save the capital without saving, you have to save for making the capital, then you can succeed in capital formation.

Once I asked a friend whose name was Pankaj Roy, "Can you tell me that where does the money from the people who have the money gets from them"? Then they said that they would have received their father. Then I asked, "Where did the money come from his father?" So he told me that "he would be found by the father of his father". Then I asked, "Where did the money come from the father of his father?" So after this question, he did not say anything but completely calm down.

Now I want to tell you people that "Where is the money received by the father of the people, this money comes from spending some money and saving some money from their earned money".

If you save, then gradually you start preparing a small capital and this one day turns into big capital. Suppose that you save a rupee every day, you can prepare a year, that is 365 days, you can make a capital of 365 rupees, by saving.

Now you can get an idea of how much money you can make in your lifetime.

One person whose name was Rajesh Gupta. The one who used to

operate a flour mill By saving a little money, he had collected millions of rupees.

Capital is created only by saving, and there is no way to make capital in this world.

One whose name was Surendra Sharma. He used to work in a company in Mumbai. And he was married. His wife's name was Mayuri Sharma. She was a fully educated domestic lady. Both (husband and wife) lived in a rented flat.

Once, when Mr. Sharma was paying rent for his flat, his wife said, "Do not you think that it is equal to the installment of a newly purchased flat". Though the flat was worth 8000 rupees, which was undoubtedly equal to the installment of a newly purchased flat.

Upon hearing this, Mr. Sharma said that "what we can do in this we are compelled to do this". On hearing this, his wife Shrimati Sharma said, "Can we not take our own private flat?" Then Mr. Sharma said, "How can we buy our own private flat from where we will fetch a lot of money for advance booking of flat". Then, Mrs. Mayuri Sharma said, "We can arrange for a huge amount through savings ".

After this he started saving and within a few months he added a huge amount of money to buy his private flat and thus he managed to buy his own private flat.

You can also make your capital by saving in a similar way.

A woman named Anita Giri. He used to wash the dishes in people's houses. His gardener's condition was not well. She was very poor and also a widowed woman, her husband Amit Giri died due to a serious illness. Her husband was a laborer who used to do construction work.

Anita Giri, who lived in a slum colony, had a son and a daughter, whose son was about twenty years old, who was older than his daughter and his younger daughter, who was sixteen years old. His eldest son studied in class XII and his younger daughter was in class IX.

Mrs. Giri had a dream that she got her son a clothing shop. Although his son used to work at a clothing store.

Her mother had ordered her to pay a large part of the money she received from her salary, deposited in her name, opened in the bank, in the current account.

The result was that gradually the amount of savings increased and in the current account one day, the principal and the interest were so high that he gave advancement of two lakh rupees to rent a shop in his city market.

And her mother also opened a current account with her name in the bank. The money that was received by washing the utensils of people's houses. Whatever money was left after running the house expenses with that money, it did not spend that money in vain. That money was deposited in the bank. For this reason, a very large capital was created in both their principal and interest.

More recently, he gave his son two lakhs of rupees to make a closet in his rented shop and to buy clothes. And in this way he made his big son a clothing shop.

So you people saw that saving is amazing, it seems like magic.

Then what are you guys thinking?

Today, you start saving and then, small savings will be turned into one day, big capital, you will not even know.

The droplets fill the pot with the drop-drop, fill the rhythm with the pitcher, fill the river with rhythm and fill the ocean from the river.

***

What if we stop the rain water? You know that,

"There will be floods in the river and the entire city will start drowning"

4

How to save money?

Savings are an art, if you know this art, you can save it. Let's shed light on the art of this saving.

You people must do something or something, that means something will definitely earn. If you believe that your earnings are worth a hundred rupees, then spend fifty rupees out of it and save the remaining fifty rupees.

In this way, you can save fifty rupees from a hundred rupees.

This topic can be understood as such that if we put hundred rupees in our purse every day and take out fifty rupees from it, then after some time hundreds of rupees will be collected in our purse.

One person whose name was Sanjeev Ram. Who was a laborer and used to lumber over a saw machine. His monthly salary was three thousand rupees and he was married. He had two sons, the elder son's name was Rajiv Ram and the younger son was named Vineet Ram.

He spent only half of his salary and saved half the part, that is, he used to spend fifteen hundred rupees in his salary and used to save fifteen hundred rupees

In this way, he had prepared a million rupees of capital in a few years.

The only source of savings is the hundred earnings - fifty expenses = fifty savings.

Keep a lifelong reminder of this form of saving. This saving formula can make you rich. And to be rich, this form of savings will always be brought into practice in our daily life.

If Tata Sons owner Late Mr. Jamshed Tata spent as much as he had earned, could he make a Tata company? In the same way, if Reliance Industries's producer Late Shri Dhirubhai Ambani did what he used to earn, would he be able to raise Reliance Industries?

In the same way, if you want to be rich then you also have to save.

If you do not save then you can not be rich. And you do not say that you earn money, but earning is that money which you saved by keeping yourself restrained.

It is a matter of ancient times. Two brothers lived in a village. One was named Sriram and the other was named Sreesama, and both of them planned to earn a large city.

Shriram did his business in millions and he earned good money but he could not save a single penny. And when he came to his village, his home, the people said about Sriram that "he went to the city and did not earn a single penny" Although Shriram had done his business in millions but still people said that " Nothing earned from business life "

Similarly, Sreesama also did his business in millions of rupees. He had done millions of rupees in his business life. But Sreesama had saved money along with earnings.

So when he came to his hometown, his home, his family members said that "Sreesama has come from abroad to earn millions of rupees."

Way of saving

If you earn 100 rupees then you spend only fifty rupees out of it and save fifty remaining rupees anywhere.

Gradually and saving fifty rupees every day your deposited capital will go on increasing day by day, and one day it will come that you will be converted into millions of Rupees and you will not have any realization.

The only way to save is to spend half the amount of earning and save half of it.

Avoid the excuse not to save money

Some people are "how we can save, whereas our earnings do not meet our mandatory expenses only and it is impossible to save in this situation".

But by saying this, we can not reject the truth and the truth is that, we do not want to give up and we do not want to suffer. Therefore, we make an excuse of compulsory expenditure and strive to avoid suffering and sacrifice.

If you do not save this kind of false pretense, you will never be able to become rich and successful.

And in the end, I would say to you people, "You see your inner soul peeking from a soft mind and ask if we really can not save".

Never do this to save money

Some people think that if our expenditure becomes one hundred rupees, if our earnings are worth two hundred rupees then we will become rich by saving.

But regrettably rarely it happens.

See a picture in this subject which is a slum colony of this world. Have you ever thought that there is a slum settlement in this world? Can people living in slums do not make their own private and permanent home?

This can of course be made a personal and a solid house, but whatever money they earn, these people blow into alcoholism, intoxication, gambling and meat. And it also thinks that when we will earn more than our expenses, we will make a personal, firm home by saving money.

to regret! It never happens that their earnings are worth more than their expenses.

Keep your population down to save money

If we have to save money, then we have to keep our population under control more. If our population is high then our expenditure will be in the same sense if we keep our population down, then our expenses will be less and we will get a better opportunity to prepare our capital. Anyway, when earnings will be low and food will be high, then how can we go ahead in this condition and in the end, I will tell the same thing to the people that keep their population under control.

Assume that if you have only one son, you have to bear the expenses of one son, but if you have ten sons, then you have to bear the expenses of ten sons and you will teach ten sons to read and write, They have to be brought up, they will have to be employed and married.

In this way, our life will be like the life of a porter and we will continue to bear the burden of whole life.

***

5

How to trade?

As all of you have been told in the last chapter, if you save fifty percent of your earnings every day, then that small savings will gradually be transformed into a very large capital and by doing business with it The background will also be built.

But when we step on the trade route, we start to feel a terrible fear that our capital should not be broken and our business fails and we can not get destroyed.

"Can you tell me why there is harm in business". So you will have the answer: "When our business does not run, we do not earn and when earnings do not occur, then our expenditure starts to break our capital and we begin to find a loss in our business."

But it is not true that there is a loss in the business due to lack of business. The truth is that the loss in the business is due to spending more than its earnings.

If you spend more than your business earning you will always take the loss.

This thing meant that you people understood that the loss of business is not due to the excessive running of the business. Loss in business is due to spending more and finally we reach the conclusion that we should decide on our own expense according to our earnings.

Assuming that Aamir Khan's earnings of one hundred rupees and his expenditure is two hundred rupees, then in this situation, Aamir Khan will lose his business. And in contrast, if Aamir Khan's earnings are worth two hundred rupees and his expenditure is one hundred rupees, then in this situation, Aamir Khan will always benefit.

The good way to do business is that if you have earned a hundred rupees, then you should take up your expenses only in fifty rupees. And fifty remaining rupees should be brought back into business.

In this situation your business will go on growing and one day you will become a very rich person.

This action looks like magic, and it works like thithi.

One person whose name was Suresh Dubey, who used to store a daily commodity. He used to spend half the amount of income from his shop and used to invest half the amount back into his business. So that his business was growing very fast. He first opened a shopping mall by collecting money from rising income. After that, he opened a school for children by collecting money from the revenue from shopping malls. After that, after collecting the money from the school income, he opened a clothing factory, and in a short time he started running the clothes factory. In this way, that person became the owner of a billionaire and several factories after a few years.

This story of Suresh Dubey also runs in ours and your business life.

Suppose that whatever Mrs. Sita earns from her business, if she spends only fifty percent of it and fifty percent of her part is back in her business, then what? You can tell me where the business of Mrs. Sita will reach one day. And in contrast, if Mrs Sita, who earns from her business and who has spent that earning, then Mrs. Sita will reach where she will be with this verse some time later.

Please note that whatever earned from your business, put it back in your business.

To be rich we have to expand our business because without big business we can not be rich, this is a true rule. Therefore, whatever we earn from our business, we should put it back in our business.

I mentioned in the story of Suresh Dubey that he used to spend half the amount of income in his daily commodity shop, and put half of his income back into his shop. If he had spent the entire amount of income from his shop, could his business grow. And when his business did not grow, could he open the shopping mall? So could he open the school? So could he open the fabric factory? Did he become the owner of a billionaire and many factories?

In the same way if you do not return the money earned from the business back into business then will your business go forward.

Apply the money earned from your business to your business, do not deposit it to the bank.

Many people deposit their money into the bank, which is very wrong. The bank will give us profitable at very slow pace. While our money in the business sector will move very fast. Therefore, by depositing money in the bank, we can not be rich because life is very short.

I have also seen that many people deposit all their money in the bank. By which their money is somewhat safe, but in this way they can become even more poor. For example, money that is spent for sickness, marriage, construction of houses or any other reason. It is not possible to return to the bank due to good business and not good earning, which eliminates all the deposits in the bank and it gets ruined.

***

<u>6</u>

<u>What is the secret of the rich?</u>

As you have learned in previous chapters, to make us rich, by saving fifty percent of our earnings, and making a big or small capital, we have to invest in any business and by this action we earn money Can be rich.

<u>Whatever money you save from your earnings, you must definitely put it in a business, this policy can make us rich</u>

Whatever money you save from your earnings, of course we have to get into any industry, otherwise you can never be rich. Listen to a story on this topic.

"Once, one person donated one kilogram of wheat to a visitor, and from that person, receiving one kilogram of wheat, the visitor was very pleased and thanked the donor very much.

After that the visitor brought one kg of wheat to his house. And he grinded wheat, made his dough, made bread, and even consumed those loaves.

But he did not grind all the wheat by grinding it, but saved some handful wheat and sowed the remaining wheat in the field.

After some time, small plants were out of the seed which were planted, and in some days the earrings were born from those plants and in a few weeks the earrings also got cooked and cut and buried."

"Now that visitor has a bag that means fifty kilograms of wheat".

To be rich, take the support of compound rule.

Do you all know about the compounding benefits, if not, then let me tell you what the compounding rule is.

Assume that you have deposited some money in any bank. This money has increased after some time with the interest paid by the bank. Now interest in our deposit money has also been added and now the bank will also pay interest on the interest added to our principal. And later on that interest will also pay interest.

This verb is called the compound benefit verb action. This topic can be understood in this way as well.

Like a farmer has a farm, then there are three crops in a year. If the farmer buys another farm by saving half of the money from the three crops, then he will have two fields and his earnings will get double. And if after some time the farmer buys another farm by saving the money in his farm, then that farmer will have three fields and his earnings will be thriving.

In this way the poor farmer, owner of a farm, will become a very rich landowner one day by this compounding rule.

Definitely saved from your earnings, money must be invested in some industry.

The money that we save from our earnings must be invested in a business, only then we can get rich. That is why we have to think about new businesses and we have to continue to gather information about trade. If we do not put our saved money in any industry, then our earnings will not increase and we will not be able to get rich.

Put your money in a business, otherwise destruction and deluge will be achieved.

If you do not apply your money to increase any business then you will definitely get the destruction and the cataclysm. So you should find opportunities to increase earnings and progress of your business.

A twin brother used to live in an unknown city, one was named Ajay and the other was named Vijay, both brothers were a high ranking businessman.

Big brother Ajay, whatever he had earned from his business, he used to spend only half of it and the remaining half of the rest, he used to put it back in his business. So his business was moving forward at a fast pace. It is a matter of time that Ajay got seriously ill and his disease was spent millions of rupees, but he did not make any financial difference because his business was huge and his earnings were very high, Something went normal.

In the same way, Vijay also earned the money from his business and deposited that money in any bank.

That's why his business did not spread much. Once Vijay was also severely sick and lakhs of rupees were spent in his illness.

Because he did not invest his earned money back into his business, due to this there was not much earning in his business. He fully spent the money deposited in the bank by himself to complete the treatment of his illness and after that the entire capital deposited in his bank ended and he got the destruction.

***

7

What to do to stay rich forever?

There will be no benefit from being rich. As long as we do not preserve our property and become rich in the situation.

For the stable wealth, we have to be cautious of our descendants (children).

After our death, the business made by us and the real estate owner will be our descendants and he will also be the protector of that property.

In this situation, they have to teach the method of expenditure and earning and they have to be well-organized about the rules of trade and economics.

If we fail to do so, then all the movable and immovable property of all the persons we have earned and will be destroyed will be destroyed by our sons (descendants).

That's why we have to be cautious of our descendants.

Open reserve account (bank)

It may be that our business is running properly and it may also be that we have enough money. But time does not always remain the same and then the Goddess of wealth is also playful.

So, even if we know all this, the life of our own and our descendants will leave the trust of fate.

No, how can we do so, then what will we do?

For this, we have to open a reserve bank account. The Reserve Bank is with every nation, the work of the Reserve Bank is to save money for the nation's emergency crisis. This Reserve Bank raises the money by the citizens of its nation, by way of tax or other forms and keeping it safe with that money, keeps growing by giving loans on interest by their subsidiaries.

So, you people have also understood the meaning of this Reserve Bank.

We should also open a reserve (bank) account and continue to accumulate money in that account. And in no case should not get any money deposited in that reserve (bank) account. So that we can compete with any kind of economic and emergency crisis.

Reserve (bank) account is the essence of stable wealth.

take out insurance

In ancient times, China was a neighboring country of our country (India) and is still there today. He built a wall for the protection of his nation, which is also called the wall of China.

The main purpose of this China's invention was to protect China against the invasion of external or neighboring countries, we would also have to resort to insurance wall to avoid the attack of economic and emergency crisis.

The insurance company will always be with us. It will stay with us till our survival and after our death our family will live together.

Therefore, insurance is a mandatory topic to achieve stable prosperity and we can not even leave this mandatory topic.

Collect Gold

Did you know that gold is a currant money and can roam it whenever you want Perhaps this is the reason that every nation in this world collects gold. Not only this, gold also cooperates with us in times of crisis. If we have it, then we can remove our grief by selling it.

The collection of gold gives us great joy and peace and strength. If our business fails and our capital gets broken, then we can sell it, reproduce our capital, and re-establish our business.

Gold is like God in the clock of crisis.

If a nation or person does not have gold, then the world calls that nation or that person poor or beggar.

Gold is the root of man's inner soul. We must always root this root.

Therefore, collect gold for steady prosperity. Gold is the foundation of the economy of any nation and of any person. This foundation should always strive to make us strong and consistent.

Friendship with rich and successful people.

Consistency of wealthy and successful individuals is essential for stable prosperity. Make fun with the falcon to become a falcon.

If you do not make friendship with rich people, you will not get help in any financial crisis because you have not made friends with rich and successful people, how can a poor and unsuitable person help you? Who does not have money

For the stable wealth, you should have something like this, that you can get help on time.

Make real estate

We should continue to buy and sell land, farms, parks and houses. If we believe that our business has lost or if our business fails for any reason, then we will be able to cultivate the farm purchased by them and earn income from them. You can build your own capital and then create your business again. Or, by pledging our farm, land, garden and home mortgage or by selling it again, we can revive our business by reproducing our capital.

Always keep progressing for stable prosperity.

If the ocean stops its motion it will definitely dry up. They know why, "Because when the ocean flows, it passes through many cities and many villages, and by this action, it keeps the water of many rivers in itself, so that the water inside it always remains filled and if it is against it If you stop your speed, the water of many rivers will not flow in it, and it will dry completely once or twice. "

Similarly if we do not move forward on the path of progress and stop the speed of our progress, then we will also get the destruction, because when we progress, we have money and our expenses keep fit, but When we do not progress, our daily spending does not stop. Since we are not progressing and our daily expenses do not stop there. In this situation, our capital starts to collapse and our fields, parks and houses are sold and we get the destruction

Therefore, to avoid destruction and to the stable eminence, always keep walking on the path of progress.

***

Do not ever do this to become rich.

Many people think that, when we have a lot of money, then we will become rich by doing business of our choice. But they do not have enough money all the time in life so that they can do any business and become rich.

There was a 35-year-old young man named Anil Sonkar who used to save the fruit. Its economic condition was not well.

It also thought in our way that when I had a lot of money, I would become rich by doing good and big business. but alas! Anil Sonkar never had enough money to do a big business and all his life went through poverty.

So do not ever do this to be rich. If we have a little or a lot of money, then try to employ it, by the same effort, we can get rich.

We do not have any business system, so how can we become rich? Avoid such excuses.

Many people come out quickly by making excuses that we do not have money, so how can we become rich in this situation? While there is a lot of money needed for business.

A person like you, whose name was Rajan Bharti. Who always thought that I do not have money, so how can I do any business? Perhaps this was the reason that Shri Bharti remained poor for whole life.

Use whatever little or more money you have with confidence.

Whatever money you have, the more or less is enough. You must have seen a huge banyan tree. Do you know that the seed of a banyan tree is like a mustard grain?

Yes, you people have heard right that the banyan tree is grown from a seed equal to a mustard.

So use whatever little or more money you have in your business with complete confidence.

There are many people in this world who have done their business in very low capital and have registered their names in the high list of the rich.

Avoid thinking that all those people who have become wealthy in this world are from business of two numbers.

Those who do not know the secret of the rich, they think. Those who are rich, they do some business of two numbers.

The same thing is known about a very wealthy merchant of this world, whose name was Sri Dhirubhai Ambani. People used to say about them that late Shri Dhirubhai Ambani had resorted to two number of wealth to become rich.

But the truth is that the late Shri Dhirubhai Ambani used to do petrol work on petrol pump when he was a teenager and from there he saved some money and after that he came to Mumbai.

Initially he started the trade of clothing here. In his time, the trend of wearing a telekat cloth in India started.

At that time there were telekat clothing factories in India. But the thread from which they were made, the thread came from abroad, these threads were called duplicate silk.

Seeing all this, late Shri Dhirubhai Ambani came to understand that if a silk yarn factory is installed then it will run very much and they did the same.

Since there was no factory of fake silk thread in India, the factory of their thread was very much running. And from here he put his first step in the corporate world.

You have to arrange the capital itself to do business.

Many people spend their entire lives waiting in this waiting that if someone gives us capital from anywhere, we will become rich by doing our business.

And rarely would it happen, that someone would ever give them capital.

Even before I thought that if I give any money to me then I will do a business. But at the moment no one has given me one rupee to do business. If you are thinking something like this then only wasting your precious time.

To get money from this world, show yourself doing business.

People bet on that horse that runs fast and the race is about to win.

In the same way, people will give us money only then. When we become a successful businessman, we will show this world.

Do you know that the bank does not lend anyone a dollar for new business. The reason for this is that you are starting a new business and if you can not run your new business, the bank's money and bank loan will sink.

So till we do not do any successful business, no relatives, any friends and even our parents will not give us money to do business.

To catch the big fish, the little fish has to make the fodder

Even if you are thinking of doing a great job or doing big business, you should continue doing any small work according to your capital. With this we will continue to earn money and the background of our great work or employment will continue. Keep in mind that for the big fish to be trapped, the small fish has to become a fodder ie small business is needed for big business.

A man named Ayush Saxena, who was of thirty years of age. The only divine dream was to open the building material shop, but he did not have any money. While opening the building material store takes millions of rupees, he started trying to make a background to realize his divine dream.

He gathered all the junk in his house and sold it to the junkyard and after that he got the money, only three hundred rupees. She started working on selling the newspaper and magazine on the sidewalk in such a way.

Gradually the time passed and its capital also increased and now the day came that Ayush Saxena's divine dream of opening the shop of building material was going to come true.

<u>Keep doing any small work, the background of doing bigger work will continue to be prepared, if you do not do it, then you will not be able to do any great work (trade).</u>

Many people keep thinking all the lives that, if we do our business then we will do great, otherwise we will not.

"Well I value their feelings, but can you tell me that where will the money come from them to do bigger work? What will be rain? "

And now you have to keep the answers to this question to me. So whatever I am saying is telling the truth: "We should continue to do any small work, this creates the background of big work".

Even if you have a lot of capital, you should not do any new business by putting more capital.

If you do your job in low capital then your business does not go, you will get experience in less money. And if you do business in a lot of capital then you will have to suffer more if your business fails. So, having more capital, do your business in lesser capital.

Always do some small business

If you continue to do any small work, you will continue to have money and you will always be happy and when you understand any major business at that time, you will do that business. And if you do not do any small work then you will not have even a single penny. And if in the meantime you understand any big business, then you will not be able to do it.

See a picture on this issue "Once upon a time, a man who was very poor and did not have any money to do any employment with him. He thought, let's become the author. Because no money has to be invested in writing, in this, only knowledge and mind are used. After this he started working hard and after seven months of hard work a book was prepared. Which was based on philosophy of life and success. The book was very good and this book could not dislike anybody. After that the man reached the publication to publish the book, then the editor was demanding thirty thousand rupees for publishing that book, and that poor writer did not even have a single penny. However, his book was not published by that publication, published by any other publication where he had not even given a rupee to get his book published ".

That's why I am telling you people that "we must always continue doing some or some small work".

Always save money from your earnings

If you do not save money from your earnings, then no business will be able to understand it.

One person named Pramod Kumar was. Which used to store electronic items. A house was sold in its neighborhood. The owner of the house wanted to go to another city because his son used to work there. He was very quick to sell his house, so that he was selling a home of Rs 30 lakh, for twenty lakh rupees. But Pramod Kumar could not buy that house because Pramod Kumar did not save money from his earnings, so he did not have the money. His loss of fifteen lakh rupees was caused by not buying his house, because the house was later sold for at least thirty five lakh rupees.

***

9

Rich formula for people with a job.

Job-seekers have a problem at all that they do not have time to do business, while business is very important to them. So that their income can grow and they can become rich.

That's why they need a business that does not take long.

Let us shed light on business that is not taking time and search for such businesses.

Work of moneylenders (act of lending on interest)

For this work, you have to save some money from your salary and collect slowly and make it a huge capital. That money should be lenders only on good interest to traders. So that he can make a profit from your capital and also return the principal with a dividend.

In this way, you can not waste time and earn good profit without any labor.

Sell and buy gold

You should buy gold by saving some money from your salary and when the price of gold increases, you should sell it, it can earn you profit.

Along with sleeping you should also trade in silver and this type of business does not take time. You can do this kind of business along with your job.

Do land, farm and home business

You should also work to buy and sell land, farm and house by making a capital by saving money from your salary for this also. You can also get rich by making profits, and the fun thing is that even in such a work time Do not think and you can do your job with pleasure.

Cultivate

If you have a farm barn, then you should cultivate fertile and if you do not have a farm then you should save money from your salary and buy a farm and cultivate it. Simultaneously, you should continue to grow your farm. By continuously growing the farm, you will become rich and do not take much time in farming. With this you can do your job comfortably.

Do cattle work

For this, by making money by saving money from your salary, you have to buy a piece of land in a village and you have to do business of goats, sheep, cow, buffalo and pig.

Do you guys know that India's ancient economy rests on cow farming.

At the time when India was called gold bird, at that time the person who had a lot of cow was considered wealthy and in the same way the Israeli economy in ancient times rested on sheep and goat farming.

Therefore, you also have to resort to animal husbandry to be financially capable.

This work does not even take time because you can do this work even with servants.

Do fish and poultry work

For this, you also have to save money from your salary, buy a puddle and do the job of fishery or you work for poultry. Both of these jobs can be done by the servants and you can do your job too much fun.

Work for tree and gardening

You will have to buy any single garden by saving money from your salary and you will have to set up timber tree such as Sagwan, Shisham Acacia and Lippas.

With this, you have to plant a fruit tree according to mango, neem, berries, litchi, guava and place and climate. This will give you double benefit. First you will earn by selling fruits and when the tree becomes dry, you will earn by selling it and selling it. So to work as a horticultural to become rich.

This work also does not take time. You can also do this work with servants too.

***

10

Whatever you do to be rich, keep moving forward. Please note, think big.

One person whose name was Rajesh Gaur, had kept a goat. Which gave two children every year. to regret! But this does not make Rajesh Gaur ever rich. What would be the benefit of having two goat children in a year? And in contrast, Manoj Pasi, who had kept twenty goats, and twenty goats produced forty children in a year.

For this reason Manoj Pasi is having fun and is living a good life.

The realization of this story is that "Whatever you do, do it on a large scale and try to push it forward. This is the essence of the rich that, go ahead and keep growing ".

Similarly, one person had a daily commodity shop. Its name was Mithilesh Agarwal, its annual income was twenty thousand rupees. But it never tried to increase its earnings and Mr. Agarwal had to spend all his life in the wages of twenty thousand rupees annually.

But Rupesh Patel, in contrast, had a daily commodity shop and he kept trying to increase his earnings. As a result today, Rupesh Patel is at the forefront of his city's rich list.

<u>Your earnings can only increase and you can be rich only when you increase your business</u>

You can be rich only when your earnings are high and you have to increase your business to increase your earnings because without big business you can not be ririh.

Spread like a fire in the forest and look at it with a vivid look

The fire in the forest spreads at very fast speed, its speed is very fast, it spreads very rapidly around the air through the air. It can not be stopped on any condition. You should also follow this forest fires as ideal.

Do any small work, but keep your thinking strong.

If you do any small job or employment, then you have to keep your thinking bigger.

One person whose name was Vimal Jalan, who used to sell ice cream on a bicycle, but he had a big idea that he wanted to set up a factory of ice cream, and for this he started trying. And one day his big thinking Turned into reality.

Similarly, a person named Raghavendra Singh was the one who used to run the Silema machine in Silema Hall. His only dream was to create his own private hall and he was looking for it, one day his dream was fulfilled.

Best wishes

www.ingramcontent.com/pod-product-compliance
Lightning Source LLC
Chambersburg PA
CBHW020543220526
45463CB00006B/2179